Maïte Roche

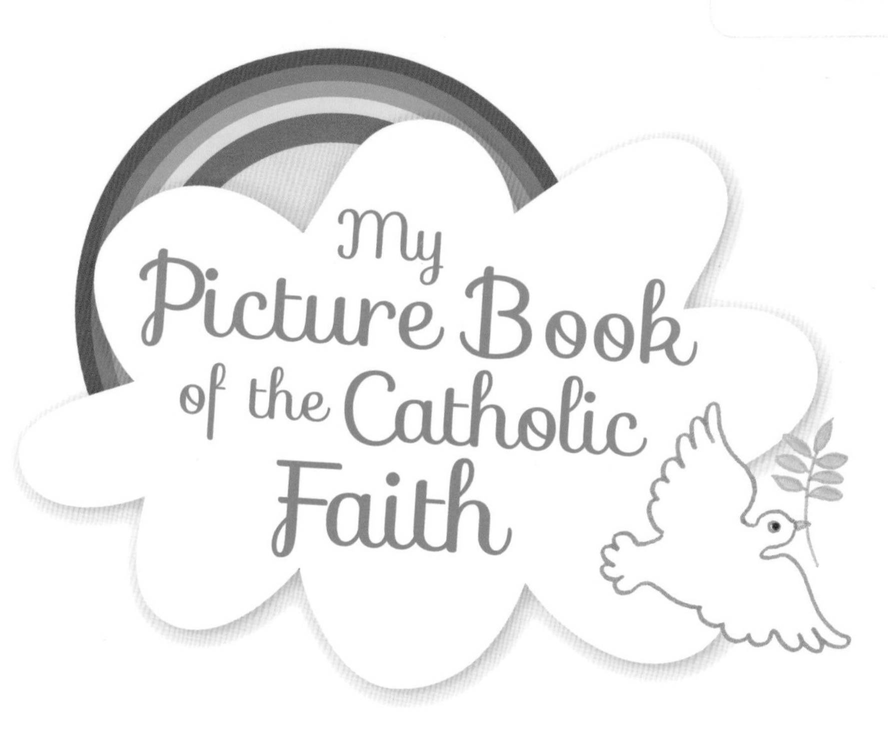

MAGNIFICAT • Ignatius

Ever since you were very little, God has loved you like a Father with a great heart. Listen to his Word, get to know him, and love him with all your heart. He invites you to enter for ever into a great story of love.

This book was written to tell you this beautiful love story. Look at the pictures and open up your ears. You will meet those who loved God before you: Noah, Abraham, Moses, David....

You will also meet Jesus. Watch him as a little child in the family of Mary and Joseph. Listen as he shares the Good News of God's love. See Jesus give his life for us.

You'll learn, too, about the sacraments of the Church. Throughout your whole life, they will unite you with Jesus and give you the strength of his love.

Celebrate with your family and with all the people of God the great seasons and feasts of the Church: Advent, Christmas, Epiphany, Lent, Palm Sunday, Easter, Ascension, Pentecost, Assumption, All Saints' Day....

Discover what it means to live as a child of God.

Contents

God Is Love

God made you and loves you.
He gave you a family to care for you.
We are all God's beloved children.
Let's thank and praise God!

Thank you, Lord, for my mommy and daddy.

Thank you for brothers
and sisters.

Thank you for grandmas
and grandpas.

God Gives Life

Thank you, Lord, for the sky and the earth, for the sun, the moon, and the stars, and for all your good and beautiful creation! "O Lord, our Lord, how great is your name in all the earth!" (Psalm 8:1).

Thank you for plants,
flowers, and fruits.

Thank you for
all the animals.

Thank you, Lord, for all the people you have made.
You created us in your image and likeness.

The Bible, the Word of God

God has made us all part of a great love story.
God invites you every day to receive his love
so that he can give you his happiness.

Adam and Eve lived happily in the garden of Eden.
God was their friend. They could eat of the tree of eternal life,
and everything was good.

God said, "Of the tree of the knowledge of good and evil you shall not eat" (Genesis 2:17). But the serpent tricked Adam and Eve, and they disobeyed God! They had to leave the garden, and their lives would be hard. But God promised that one day he would send the Savior.

God's Covenant with Noah

God saw that many people were wicked.
He chose a good and just man called Noah and said to him,
"Build an ark to shelter yourself and your family,
and two animals of every kind." Noah did as God told him.
Then it rained for forty days: it was the flood!

The dove brought back an olive branch in its beak.

God blessed Noah and his family, saying,
"Behold this rainbow: it is the sign of my covenant of love
with you for ever" (Genesis 9:13).

God Makes a Promise to Abraham

God called to Abraham, "Leave your home and your country and go to the land that I will show you. I will make of you a great nation. Look up and count the number of the stars if you can: your descendants will be as numerous as the stars in the sky" (Genesis 12:1-2 and 15:5).

Abraham trusted in God. So he set off for the Promised Land with his wife, Sarah, his servants, and his flocks.

You too are part of the great family of Abraham. You are like a star shining in the heart of God.

God Frees His People through Moses

Before they left Egypt, families shared the Passover meal in honor of God who frees his people.

In the desert, God took care of his people. He gave them manna, their daily bread. He gave them his law so they would love him with all their heart and live together in peace; these are the Ten Commandments that God gave to Moses. You too can learn to love God with all your heart and to live in peace with others.

God Chooses David

David was a young shepherd of Bethlehem. He played the harp and sang his prayers as he watched over his sheep. God chose him to become king and lead his people. You too can sing with David: "The Lord is my shepherd, I shall not want" (Psalm 23:1).

With his slingshot and five little stones, David beat Goliath, a giant in the enemy army, for God was with him.

When he became king, David danced before the ark of the covenant that held the Ten Commandments of God. It was carried to Jerusalem. His son Solomon would have a great Temple built there for God.

God Promises a Savior

The people forgot about the love of God and strayed away from him. There were wars, and many were taken prisoner. So God called prophets to give his unhappy people hope again. Isaiah said, "Here am I! Send me" (Isaiah 6:8).

Isaiah said, "Rejoice, a Savior will be born. A young woman will give birth to a son. He will be of the family of David" (Isaiah 7:14).

God said to the Prophet Jeremiah, "I will make a new covenant. I will place my law in their hearts, and all will know me, from the littlest to the greatest" (Jeremiah 31:33-34).

The Annunciation to Mary

The angel Gabriel was sent by God: "Hail, Mary, God has chosen you to be the mother of the Savior, Jesus, the Son of God, by the power of the Holy Spirit" (Luke 1:26-35). Thank you, Mary, for saying yes to God. Blessed are you among women.

“Listen, Joseph. Mary is expecting the Savior promised by God. You will call him Jesus” (Matthew 1:18-23).

Mary and Joseph trusted God and awaited the birth of Jesus.

God Gives Us His Son

It's Christmas night. Little baby Jesus, lying in the manger next to Joseph and Mary, you bring us the peace and the joy of God.

"Rejoice, a Savior is born to us! Glory to God in the highest, and on earth peace to people of good will!" (Luke 2:14).

You can welcome Jesus, too. He reaches out his arms to you to give you all his love.

The Adoration of the Magi

By following a star, the Magi found Jesus and Mary. They were filled with joy. They fell on their knees before Jesus and offered him their gifts of gold, frankincense, and myrrh.

The Presentation in the Temple

Mary and Joseph presented Jesus in the Temple of Jerusalem. Through the grace of the Holy Spirit, old Simeon recognized Jesus as the Savior, the Light of the world, for whom he had been waiting. He was filled with joy!

The Holy Family

Look at Jesus, Mary, and Joseph at home in Nazareth.
They care for each other, united in the love of God.
"Jesus grew in strength and wisdom,
and the grace of God was with him" (Luke 2:52).

Jesus prayed with his family and grew up with the other children of his village.

At the age of twelve, Jesus surprised the scribes in the Temple with his intelligence. Mary and Joseph went looking for him. He said to them, "Did you not know that I must be in my Father's house?" (Luke 2:49).

The Baptism of Jesus

When he was thirty, Jesus was baptized by John the Baptist.
The Holy Spirit came down from the sky as a dove,
and God said, "This is my beloved Son,
with whom I am well pleased" (Matthew 3:17).

Jesus prayed in the desert for forty days.
He was preparing to share the Good News of God's love.

Jesus called Twelve Apostles: "Follow me!" (Matthew 4:19).
Jesus calls you, too, to know him and to love him.
Do you want to be his friend?

Jesus Shares the Good News

Jesus said, “Blessed are the poor, for God takes care of them; blessed are those who weep, for God comforts them” (Matthew 5:3-4). Lord, open my ears to hear your Word. Open my eyes to see your wonders.

To those who come to Jesus, he gives life.
"The deaf hear, the blind see, the poor have the Good News preached to them" (Luke 7:22).

Lord, if you wish to, you can heal me.

Jesus Teaches Us How to Pray

Let's pray to God our Father in the way Jesus taught us. It is the prayer of the children of God.

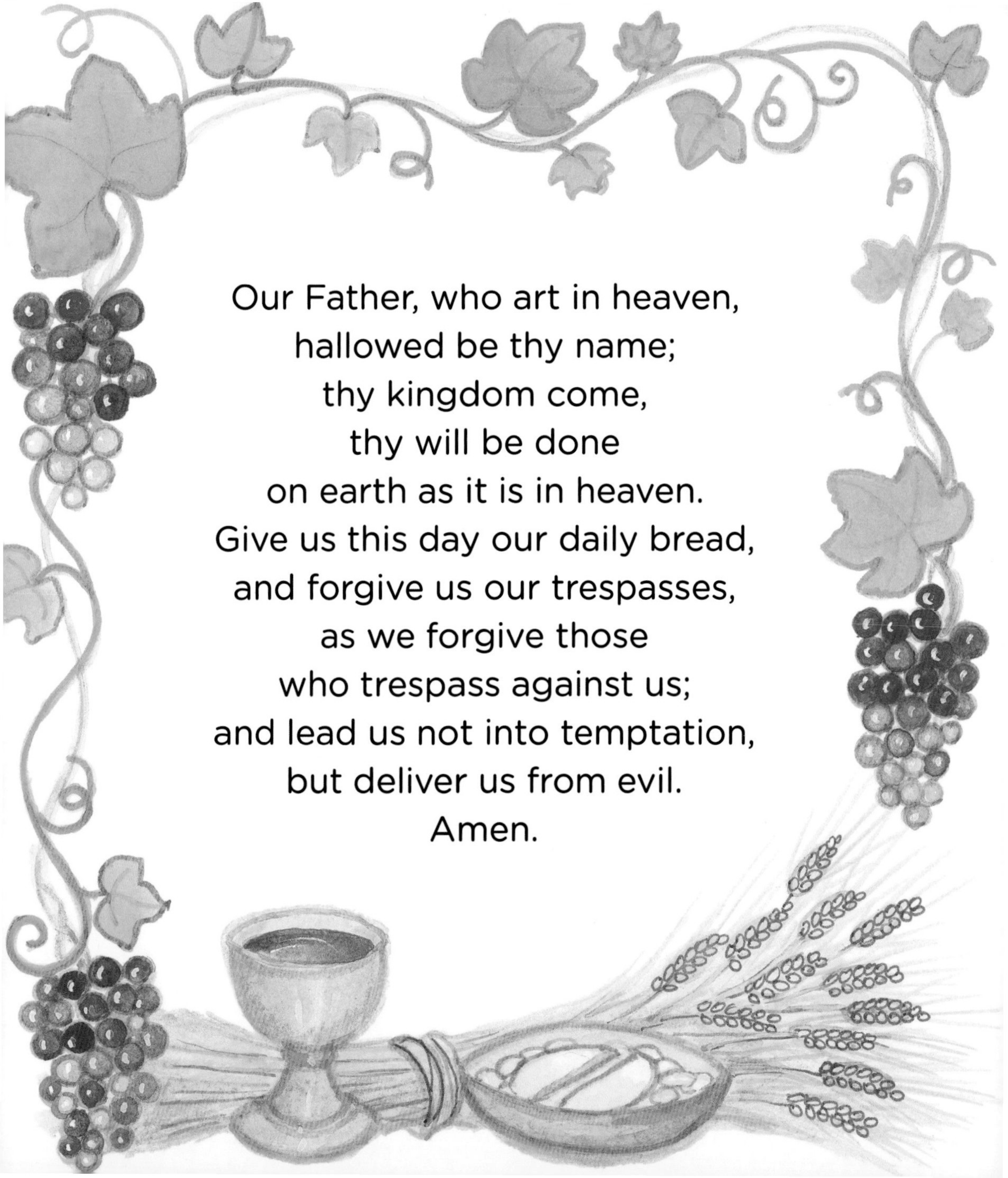

Our Father, who art in heaven,
hallowed be thy name;
thy kingdom come,
thy will be done
on earth as it is in heaven.
Give us this day our daily bread,
and forgive us our trespasses,
as we forgive those
who trespass against us;
and lead us not into temptation,
but deliver us from evil.
Amen.

The New Covenant of Love

Jesus entered Jerusalem. "Hosanna! Blessed is he who comes in the name of the Lord!"

Jesus invited his Apostles to his Last Supper. Before the meal, he washed their feet, to teach them to serve each other.

During the meal, Jesus blessed the bread, broke it, and gave it to them, saying, “This bread is my body which will be given up for you.” Then he blessed the wine and gave it to them, saying, “This wine is my blood which will be poured out for you” (Matthew 26:26-29).

“I give you a new commandment: love one another as I have loved you” (John 15:12).

Jesus Gives His Life on the Cross

Taken away by soldiers and crowned with thorns, Jesus carried the heavy cross. Thank you, Jesus; your love is so great, you brought us God's forgiveness. "Greater love has no man than this, that a man lay down his life for his friends" (John 15:13).

Thank you, Jesus, for giving up your life out of love, and for giving us Mary as our Mother.

What great sorrow was in the heart of Mary when Jesus was laid in the tomb!

Easter Joy

On Easter morning, the tomb was open and an angel said, "Jesus is risen! He is alive for ever!" Thank you, Jesus, for opening for us the path to eternal life in God. Alleluia!

The Risen Jesus said to Mary Magdalene,
"I am going to my Father and your Father, to my God and your God" (John 20:17).

What great joy in the hearts of Mary and the friends of Jesus when he appeared in their midst. He said to them, "Peace be with you" (John 20:19).

God Sends Us His Holy Spirit

Forty days after Easter, Jesus said to his Apostles, "You are going to receive the power of the Holy Spirit, and you will be my witnesses to the ends of the earth" (Acts 1:8). Then he disappeared before their eyes to join God his Father and to prepare a place for us in heaven.

On the day of Pentecost, the Apostles were praying with Mary.
Tongues of fire came down to rest over each of them.
They were filled with the Holy Spirit.

Three thousand people were baptized that same day.
With the power of the Holy Spirit, the Apostles went
everywhere, proclaiming the Good News.

The Beginning of the Church

Listening to the Apostles

Sharing

Praying

Breaking the bread

There were more and more Christians. They listened to the Apostles, who taught them the words of Jesus. They prayed with one heart. They broke bread together, as Jesus commanded. They shared with one another.

Peter was the first pope, the head of the Church.

Paul spread the Good News about Jesus in faraway countries.

The Church grew. Matthew, Mark, Luke, and John wrote the Gospels to make Jesus known. The Word of God spread the world over.

Welcome to the House of God

The whole Church celebrates when someone is baptized into the great family of God. Perhaps you were baptized when you were very little. If not, you can ask to be baptized when you grow up.

Here we are, Lord!

On the day of your baptism, the priest welcomes you into the Church: he calls you by name. He makes the sign of the cross on your forehead: in the name of the Father, and of the Son, and of the Holy Spirit.

Baptism

Through baptism, you receive new life in Jesus and the gifts of his Holy Spirit. The priest pours water over your forehead, saying, "I baptize you in the name of the Father, and of the Son, and of the Holy Spirit." And you are made a child of God.

You are anointed with holy oil and are clothed in white,
because you are now living in the light of Jesus.
Your godfather or godmother lights your baptismal candle.

"Blessed Virgin Mary, guide us along the path of life
and lead us to Jesus, your beloved Son."

Come, Begin the Journey

Thank you, my God, for the life you give us.
Help us to grow together in faith, hope, and love
so that we can spread your Kingdom throughout the world.

"Let the children come to me," said Jesus.

"The kingdom of God belongs to children and those like them" (Luke 18:16).

The Lord Hears Our Prayers

Jesus, Mary, and Joseph, bless my family
and all those around me. Teach us to live as you did,
in the love of God and of our brothers and sisters.

Jesus, I offer you my joys, my sorrows, and my efforts each day.

Great is the Lord. My whole heart sings to God!

Learn to Love as Jesus Does

Please, Jesus, teach me to love the way you do.
Open my hands to share.

Let's be of service to one another.

Happiness grows when it is shared.

Forgiveness

Forgive us, Jesus, for fighting, for not telling the truth,
for not sharing. Teach us how to make up
and to live together in the peace and the joy of God.

How good it is to forgive and to be forgiven!
Joy is reborn in our hearts! Thank you, Lord!

When you get older, you will be able to confess to a priest.
He will grant you God's forgiveness. It will free you and heal you
so that you can live in the joy of the children of God.

Sunday, the Lord's Day

Jesus asks us to gather together. We go to Mass.
We thank and praise God. People of God,
walk joyously, for the Lord is with you.

Make a sign of the cross: in the name of the Father,
and of the Son, and of the Holy Spirit.

Listen to the Word of God.

Blessed Are Those Called to the Supper of the Lamb

The priest says the words of Jesus: "This is my Body, which will be given up for you." "This is my Blood, which will be poured out for you." Jesus, I adore you: "My Lord and my God."

The Chalice of salvation and the Bread of life.

Let's say the prayer of the children
of God that Jesus taught us: Our Father…

Communion

At your First Communion, you will receive Jesus in the Host for the first time. It is a day of celebration. The Risen Jesus enters you and gives you all his love, his whole life, and all his strength for you to live united with God and with the Church throughout the world. After that day, you can receive Communion as often as you like. If you haven't yet made your First Communion, cross your arms over your heart so that the priest can bless you.

“The Body of Christ.” “Amen.”

Jesus, prepare my heart
to receive you.

Thank you, Jesus, I love you.

Confirmation

When you are older, on the day of your confirmation, you will receive the strength of the Holy Spirit to witness to the love of Jesus, just as the Apostles did at Pentecost.

The bishop anoints the forehead of the person to be confirmed with holy oil, saying, “Be sealed with the gift of the Holy Spirit.”

Holy Spirit, fill my heart with your gifts. Give me the joy of knowing my vocation in the service of God and the strength to carry it out.

Marriage

The bride and the groom promise to love one another
their whole lives, just like God, who loves us for ever.
Their family and friends come to share this joyous day.
Lord, bless and accompany this new family that has just begun.

The spouses say yes to one another: “I give myself to you, and I promise to love you faithfully my whole life long.” The priest gives them God’s blessing.

The newlyweds exchange wedding rings as a sign of their love and fidelity.

The Ordination of Priests

On the day of his ordination, the priest says to God, "Here I am!" He promises to live as Jesus did, at the service of others in the Church. Through the laying on of the bishop's hands and the anointing with the holy oil, he receives the power of the Holy Spirit to fulfill his mission.

Following in the footsteps of the Apostle Peter, the pope leads the people of God. The other bishops and priests help him.

The Lord calls many other men and women to live just as he did. They live simple lives of prayer and service.

The Anointing of the Sick

The priest lays his hands on the sick person and anoints his forehead with holy oil. He asks God for healing, of soul and body, and God, in his love and tenderness, always sends the sick person the strength of the Holy Spirit to be brave and patient, and to hope in his goodness.

Let's be messengers of God's tenderness.

Blessed Mary, our Mother, receive the prayers
of all those who are suffering.

The Season of Advent and the Feast of Christmas

Jesus, I await you. My heart is like a manger ready
to receive you. Welcome, Jesus! You are the greatest gift of all.
Merry Christmas! (see pages 28 and 29)

The light of the Advent wreath grows brighter every Sunday.

The Christmas tree is like the tree of eternal life in the garden of Eden. Its wood is like the wood of the cross that won eternal life for us.

Let's pray before the Nativity scene with its little figurines.

Epiphany

We share the joy of the Magi when they found baby Jesus (see page 30). Bake a king cake to remember their journey. The one who finds the hidden item is king or queen for the day!

Candlemas, the Feast of the Presentation

On Candlemas, pancakes as round as the sun are eaten in some places to forget about winter. Candles are blessed and lit because when Jesus was presented in the Temple, old Simeon saw that he was "the light of the world" (see page 31).

Jesus, may your light shine over the whole world
and guide us to you.

Living Out Lent

Ash Wednesday is the first day of Lent. "Repent, and believe in the Gospel!" says the priest as he makes the sign of the cross in ashes on our foreheads. Just as Jesus prayed in the desert for forty days, let us set off on the forty days to Easter.

Jesus, I offer you all my efforts each day.

Jesus, you said, "Love one another as I have loved you" (John 15:12). Jesus, teach me to be more like you and to love the way you do.

Palm Sunday and Holy Week

In procession, we sing out our joy at welcoming Jesus: "Holy, holy, holy Lord! Blessed is he who comes in the name of the Lord! Hosanna in the highest!" The priest blesses the palms that we will keep in our homes as a sign of the hope of the Resurrection (see page 40).

On Holy Thursday, we remember Jesus' Last Supper, when he asked his friends to be of service to others and gave us the Eucharist so he could remain present among us for ever (see pages 40 and 41).

On Good Friday, we recall Jesus' Passion and his death on the cross. Thank you, Jesus, for freeing us from sin, which makes us unhappy: "Behold the wood of the Cross, on which hung the salvation of the world" (see pages 42 to 43).

The Ascension

“Clap your hands, all peoples! Shout to God with loud songs of joy!” (Psalm 47:1). The Risen Jesus has entered into the glory of God the Father and opens to us the path to his Kingdom (see page 46).

On Holy Thursday, we remember Jesus' Last Supper, when he asked his friends to be of service to others and gave us the Eucharist so he could remain present among us for ever (see pages 40 and 41).

On Good Friday, we recall Jesus' Passion and his death on the cross. Thank you, Jesus, for freeing us from sin, which makes us unhappy: "Behold the wood of the Cross, on which hung the salvation of the world" (see pages 42 to 43).

Easter, the Greatest Feast Day

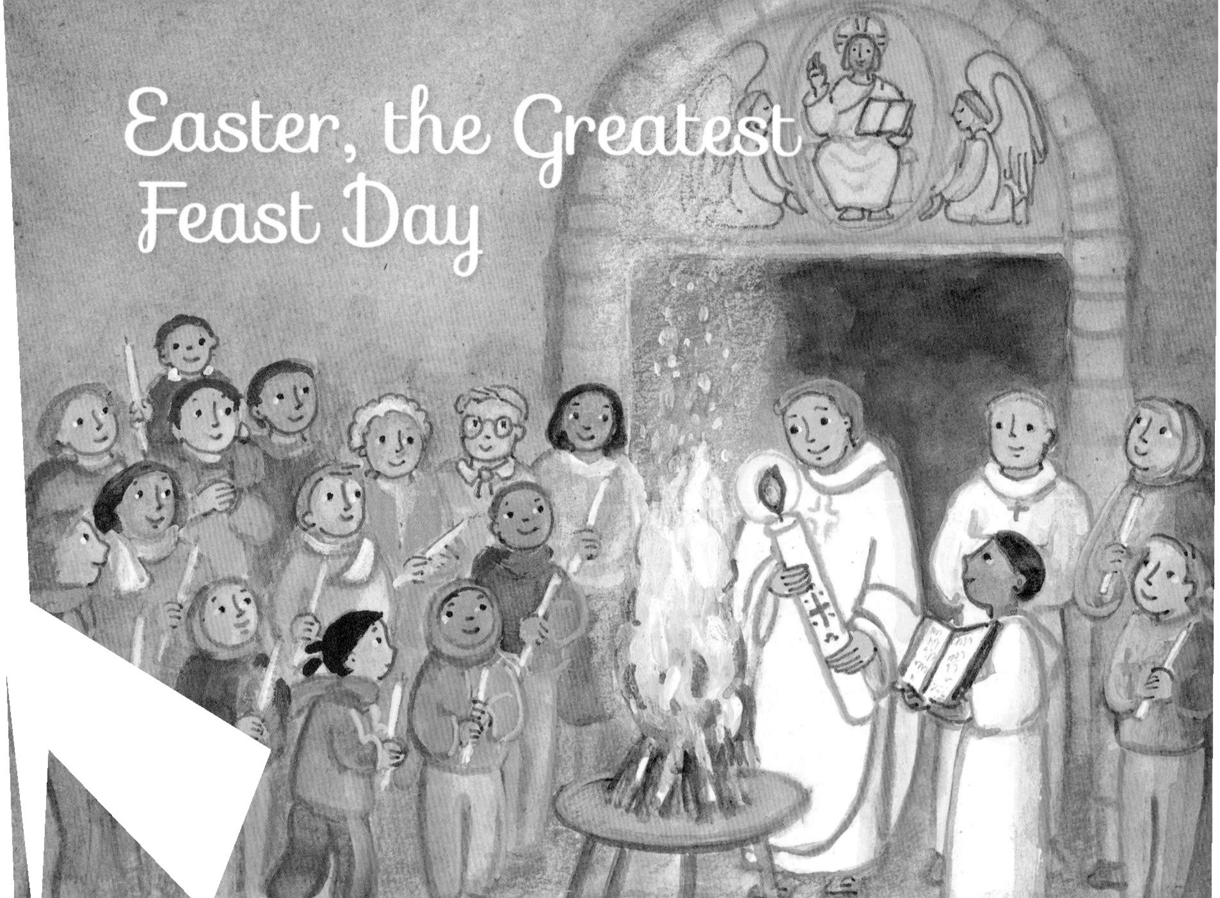

During Easter night, we celebrate the Resurrection of Jesus. The priest blesses the fire and lights the paschal candle. Its flame in turn lights all the candles, like the light of the Risen Jesus that enlightens the world. Alleluia! We are full of joy. Alleluia! (see pages 44 to 45)

The Light of Christ! Thanks be to God!

Every little Easter egg is like a promise of life.

The Ascension

“Clap your hands, all peoples! Shout to God with loud songs of joy!” (Psalm 47:1). The Risen Jesus has entered into the glory of God the Father and opens to us the path to his Kingdom (see page 46).

“I am with you always, until the end of time,” said Jesus (Matthew 28:20).

“Where two or three are gathered in my name, there am I in the midst of them” (Matthew 18:20). Lord, give me a heart full of joy and hope.

Pentecost

Gathered together through the Holy Spirit,
we are the people of God, the Body of Jesus Christ
(see page 47). "O Lord, send forth your Spirit
and renew the face of the earth" (Psalm 104:30).

Holy Spirit, fill my heart with the fruits of your love.

Blow, Spirit of God!

The Assumption

Rejoice, O Blessed Virgin Mary! Jesus received you into the light of his glory. You, the first disciple, lead us to Jesus and toward eternal joy with God our Father.

Hail Mary, full of grace,
the Lord is with thee.
Blessed art thou among women
and blessed is the fruit of thy womb, Jesus.
Holy Mary, Mother of God,
pray for us sinners
now and at the hour of our death.
Amen.

All Saints' Day

We celebrate all the saints who followed Jesus!
They show us the pathway to God. Jesus invites you, too, to love him every day in order to enter into the happiness of the children of God.

Saints of God, pray for us.

Let us pray for those who have left us in the hope of being reunited one day in the Kingdom of God.

Christ the King

Let us give glory to the Father almighty, to his Son, Jesus Christ the Lord, and to the Spirit who dwells in our hearts for ever and ever. Amen.